*ON WINGS
MADE OF GAUZE*

ON WINGS

MADE OF

GAUZE

NIKKY FINNEY

William Morrow and Company, Inc.
New York

Library of Congress Cataloging in Publication Data

Finney, Nikky.
    On wings made of gauze.

    Poems.
    I. Title.
PS3556.I53O5   1985   811'.54   84-29498
ISBN 0-688-04796-3
ISBN 0-688-05946-5 (pbk.)

Printed in the United States of America

First Edition

1 2 3 4 5 6 7 8 9 10

BOOK DESIGN BY ANN GOLD

for my aunt anna
who saved laughter and lip kisses for me
whose arms i long planned to steal then stow
under pillows or floorboards
when i grew too old, too tall to ask for them
who took my hand
and locked shoulders around me
when the world made a move for my heart
you there
throwing sky kisses to me now
i miss you so

ACKNOWLEDGMENTS

In a private huddle I assembled all of my fallen ancestors, those three hundred years and those thirty. I asked, "Please tell me how to properly thank the ones responsible for my wholeness and for this book of words." They answered, "Remember who put pencils in your hand, not promises near your heart."

Mostly, to Mama and Papa, Chip and Jerry, who claim me as only daughter and only sister, give my life place, sound and 297 flavors. But also Kamili, who red-marked my first poem and wrote "try again" at the top. Toni Cade Bambara and The Pamoja Writing Guild, for asking me every month, "So what's the plan?" and caring that I followed it. Gloria Wade-Gayles, who pointed to my hands when I screamed about the world being so unfair, who pointed to my hands when I ached with helplessness, who after a good Alabama cry pointed to my hands and whispered, "Now tell me how you feel."

Ellen Sumter, for answering the phone, for listening, loving the South and tofu as much as I. Eunice Riedel, whose special sensibilities as an editor cast her golden in my eyes. Shay Youngblood, for staying close. Tiny Laster, "Chicago" Harvey, Mr. John Henry, Mr. Cap, Mr. John Jemison, and Mr. Hi-Pockets, for being Black and men and tender. Byllye Avery and The National Black Women's Health Project, who hugged me in off the streets and gave me and my typewriter a chance. Nikki Giovanni, who never stopped believing.

And Talladega College, for loaning me her oak trees and grassy knolls where most of these poems found their altitude.

N.F.

CONTENTS

9

*ON WINGS
MADE OF GAUZE*

THE LAST FABLE:
AN INTRODUCTION

once
a younger girl
stood on a shore
of The shore
of some great ocean
and wished asked
to be much less noticeable
and far more common
she wanted three hands
an extra one for running
and no eyes
she coveted a place
a simple anywhere place
where no one would ever come to visit
or come to leave
and if they did
would not think her beauty
such an uncommon gift
always to be lauded upon
or made mention of
and far beyond anything else
she asked craved
to be allowed to remember
only older insightful things
which she offered to her spirit
with prayer and meditation

and then she whispered her desires
to those whose job it was
to hear such things
to those greatest names
with those largest ears
and they rose high
upon their most magnificent legs

13

saved for occasions of decision
and instead
led her completely away
without so much as a struggle
without so little as a blink
because hers
as they saw it
was an impossible wish
for the world
as she thought it
and as they knew it
they cared about her
and thought it best
to spare her
the eternal frustration
desiring such desires was not so uncommon
not so unusual
but granting such
was next to unheard of
and though such bestowing
was within their power
it was certainly not within their policy
so rather than tell her
what they had decided
rather than call her to their sides
to explain
instead
they had her washed away
completely and without a trace
"To save her the pain, the disappointment.
Everyone," they insisted, "does not accept what is
possible as well as the rest of us."

CHARIOTS

tall sturdy emphatic stately big-boned brown-eyed soft-
    browed
women
gingerly wrinkled
who knew no compromise and expected no favors
whose hair flowed upward in heavenly motions

women dark like mourning
and lonely
like slave songs that kept us strong

women who captured the profiles of their mothers
in lips that agitated smiles
in cheeks that refused to be turned
women
who heard the silent weeping
their fathers concealed in the straightness of their backs

women who grew from the loins of the earth
in tender mesmerizing ways
who parted the ground and stubbornly flung their souls
toward the heavens
fastening themselves to clouds
to stars
and to the sun
daring it to set on them

methodic women
earth-colored women
Black women with lean-your-head-on-my-shoulder eyes
your riches lie in state
and we pass by
not as mourners but as believers
as pursuers of your chariots
that have long lit the sky

GROCERIES

mama said
"be assertive girl and do things before people tell you"
and i always did
and she began to smile at me
and i began to smile back
at me
and bask in the sight and smell
of her easiness
cause through the years
mama had grown hard and away from youth
and away from me
but i reached for her
and she reached back
and forgot about being young
and eased into her fourth decade
and i forgot
rebelling
and remembered
the warmth of unexpected kisses
and began helping her carry grocery bags
brothers carry identities
and my father carry us all

BEARDED WALLS

brick walls be Black women
protecting   shielding
standing strong and enduring
wavelike lappings across the face

the waves that lash rhythmically against
brick   concrete
under docks and piers
be sisters wiping way tears
face to face
brick walls
no Black women never lash back

Black women
not brick walls can be heard crying
sometimes sisters be like house slippers
gently eased into
soft
but only after constant use
bought   for primary sources of relief/comfort
used   as secondary sources of importance/necessity

Black women be long
be dangling like earrings
symmetrical   complementing
brick walls shed no tears
they weep with the wind
never crying
Black women cry
walls whimper
through their sun eyes
which are peepholes that young Black boys have made
during summer baseball days/nights

Black women heal
growing back into themselves
intuitively/instinctively
preparing for other hurts
by forgiving
Black women do not forget
never remembering how

Black women be like sheets
hanging on lifelines

17

flapping where there is no wind
drying by the sun
where there is no warmth
they hold their own
fiery-eyed/positioned
waiting

brick walls
and saltwater waves have no attraction
have no similarities
do not understand each other
brick walls collapse
give up/in/out
because of salt   because of water   because of time

Black women
and saltwater tears
attract   fit   are as one
melt together
Black women made from salted water
there is no illusion
women longing
between two worlds
having to straddle   suffer   be silent
be the difference that balances survival

Black women be sensitive
to men only
who grow Black
who grow on
in Black women
Black men are like beards
needing to be stroked   smoothed   paid attention to
beardlike
needing to be trimmed
if allowed to grow
uncontested   uncontrolled   uncommitted
beards grow covering things
smiles

muffling laughter
Black men are like beards
can cover   encompass   strangle   brick walls
if ignored   if forgotten
Black men be like beards
brick walls be like Black women

‾‾
v v v

THE PREDICTORS

not yet old women
whose lives are spent
before mirrors
brushing   coloring   combing through
smoothing out
filling an emptiness
that is never filled
carrying faces like anchors
by their sides
refusing to see
how awkward a limp they've acquired
deliberately covering
smooth blue indigo cheeks
with a crimson and silver madness

princesses
descendants of egyptian crowns
spend mornings polishing   floors
and evenings starching cuffs
singing to a rhythm stubborn
that other lives
could not imitate
dare even keep harmony with

just now old women
in twice-mended stockings

move
sunspotted and sore
with pinned-up braids
pulled away from the grace of their necks
move
toward staunched shifty-eyed gentle men
tarnished brilliantly by the sun

and together they grow
hoarding the secret of muscadine wine
and the proper way of handling new fruit
they know when honeysuckles are about to bloom
and casually predict the end of the world

but no one listens
for they are merely wobbly old caricatures
from another time
discarded by this world
and all its
recentness

v v v v

UNCLES

mahogany men
with massive hands and broad mustaches
who outlived wars
and married feisty oak-imaged women
be tight with money
tender of heart
and close to me

a gallery of fathers
each of whom planted me

in the well-kept gardens
of their youth
moistened the soil
with vintage tobacco juice
and asked only that i listen
and grow to the rhythms therein

men of mahogany
and oak blossoms
who relaxed late in life
and understood that leaning
was because of trust
not weakness
men who though not supposed to
protected   shielded
their oaks
because as they taught me
love is never what it's supposed to be

THE SCRIPTURE

in my father's house
there are no mansions
winding staircases are lined with burlap
there is no gold
no silver
riches abound in the untampered darkness
absolute and undisturbed
and in the sweetness of things unknown

upon entering
all light is absorbed
there is nothing to reflect upon
no past to be remembered
no future to foresee
in my father's house

it is that house
where my mother's eyes found their sparkle
they have always sparkled
always
they have lit the way
for me
for my father
when there was nothing else that dare shine
in his presence
there has always been the presence
of my mother's eyes

now that too is uncertain
more and more
she tilts her head
upward
closing her life to moan-filled melodies
her eyes are heavy
heavy for the sight of my father
descending burlap-covered stairs
singing "melancholy baby"
he left
disappointed about
all he had not become

gone away
to assume the leading role
in a final dream
a tragedy of sorts
a comedy of sorts
but finally his own script

v v v v

NANU'S SON: FOR PAPA

yesterdays
are remembered
as years filled with nancy drew books
and nickel freeze pops
tender wishful moments for hair like my brothers'
playful days with four-legged friends
and uneasy spells
when papa was gone for such long times

v v v v

JAMES WILLIS DIED

their flashing lights
and sirened sounds
don't save everyone
their block-long trucks
and spotted dogs
don't douse
or bark
just any fire out
their laddered men
don't lie against just any wall
to lift just any child
free

some tires and people
hesitate
on unpaved   no sidewalk
but-it's-not-on-our-map
streets

they miss
picking us up
putting it out
saving us
pass right by
don't even know we're there

the unzoned
with no districts
or lines of demarcation
we live
too far out
stay too far in
look and act too much alike
aren't where we're supposed to be
yet we're where they put us
on short potholed avenues
we renamed
for kings and dukes
and baseball diamonds
and great black hopes

they take their time
as if we don't
hurt as much
bleed as red
die as quick

by the time they come
we've run for the oxygen jars
that line our cellar shelves
alongside the peach and fig preserves
and made ladders from our hair

vvvv

WOMAN TITHE 1

women
viscerally loved
now a heartbeat away
who gave us the privilege
of not hating white
and the audacity
to love Black
the right to be angry
and the choice
of braiding our hair
to arching our eyebrows
women you
you carry us through

vvvv

WOMAN TITHE 2

woman
with brownstoned polished knees
who by day
knelt
and drew pictures in the sand
and who by night
and high tide
went back out alone
to gather them
carefully
so as not to lose one ocean pasty line
then hung them in effigy
near our hearts

making tenure with life
the strength
never to be taken away
woman
you
you carry us through

‾‾‾‾
v v v v

EMPTY SOCKETS:
FOR MICHAEL STEWART

*On September 15, 1983 in New York City, Michael Stewart was
arrested for allegedly scribbling graffiti on a subway station wall.
Thirty-two minutes after his arrest he was admitted to Bellevue
Hospital in a comatose state. Thirteen days later, he died. Eight out of
the eleven Transit Authority Police were given total immunity from
prosecution. During the autopsy Michael's eyes were uncharacteristically
removed and soaked in a formaldehyde solution, which in effect washes
out any signs of hemorrhaging, which could have been used as evidence.*

stole
your eyes
so you couldn't take
the pictures with you
to those
who really matter

of their faces
centered on an iris brown
twenty-two swinging arms
in a cornea's shadow
one hundred ten
hammering fingers
off a frozen pupil's wall
which way sharp

their noses pointed
away from you
black blood
how it stains
blue boys
Blue
cut them out
so that once past
gates of pearl
and angel wings
you couldn't tell
couldn't see to tell
their mothers
baby sisters
sit on their grandmother's knee
with the word
of which one of you
brother sons
it was
while pointing to
empty sockets
that your mama
use to winterize
with Vaseline and kiss
that your papa
in the night
leaned to touch
when he didn't say
but meant
my boy
i'm with you
even when you sleep

SOUTH

here
the old one's smile is bright
anchor sure
there is no running in at dark
to prepare the heart
for a nightly fear
windows sit agape
never barred
no not them
they sit out
in the lightning's path
wanting it
warming
already flushed lives
attracting
the feared strike
daring its flash closer
to singe
what the educated call
a madness that comes with years
and enlightened ones know as
an understanding
between antiquated friends

THE UNCLAIMED

for all the ones
whose names do not ripple in neon lights
or whose distinctiveness
has yet to be embedded on printed pages

for all of you
who were never allowed moments free
to glance into mirrors
long enough to brush away
the moistness from eyes

for you
who never had time
to manicure
or massage
or lotion yourselves
all of what i am
is you

for all the songs you sang
over stovetops
and beside washtubs
that went unscored
for all the poems you scribbled
on matchbox covers
and dinner napkins
that went unpublished
unnoticed
for the many undiscovered roles
you played
in unrecorded and forgotten movies

for all that you were
for all that you always wanted to be
each time i sign my name
know that it is for a thousand like you
who could not hold a pen
but who instead held me
and rocked me gently
to the creative rhythms
i now live by

THE VENDOR

she was the color of holiday nog
on an ordinary day
old and creamy
inside years that kissed seventy
easily
she was yellow and spotted
and hopscotched on the cobblestones
in the street
where she walked and worked
the corner of
7th and U
as if the broken concrete
had been born to her
encased in the scent
of sweet rum and nuts
she moved swiftly
canvassing corners
for would-be buyers of her wares
"twenty cents a bag"
was all she ever said
and her faithfuls would appear
in pursuit of her riches
both boiled and roasted
in quest of her love
warmed over
and sometimes musty

FROM THE MOTHERS
OF WRITERS

from their very first steps
these almost women
are learned resistance
as they begin to grow
move   change   cling
hands move first
exercises taught early
to strengthen phalangeal muscles
strengthen more
medullas
cerebrums
cerebellums
move to
confusing the myth
they did not ask to be born with
so when almost women
schooled early in the course of resistance
do not do so
rebel in other directions
become unexpectedly
soft and feminine
allow finger muscles to lean back
into a forgotten misplaced girlishness
and choose double dutch
to fountain pens
their mothers weep
but never into their hands

FOR SHE WHOSE FEET
HAVE BEEN GUIDED

the combination
of afrikan men and indian summers
has colored your face a smooth but bitter black
etched the brashness in your voice
and generated much love strength

there is a rhythm into being you
a spontaneity to life itself
words be your life rhythms
having invaded your innocence years ago
becoming
where pacifiers should have been
where alphabet blocks did not fit
where simplicity
was consciously complicated
rhythms be flowing in you
in your wearing dresses
in your picking flowers
in your shifting gears
in your sweater wearing
in your zipping boots
in your popping gum
in your eyes
there be rhythmic gesticulations
rhythms be talking from the force of your stride
from the fury of your walk
from the very center of your sapphireness

seeing you
noticing how you come
"sometimes as a woman only"
humbled by one man's presence
and softened by wet kisses
from the slippery lips of those who call you "mummy"

pushing yourself
testing others
and again you come
always as a woman
only
basted in blackness
sautéed in beauty
slipped in a batter of pride
seasoned mildly nature's way
you be the reflection in life's mirror
you
the pulchritudinous rhythm that optically returns

your stories are rhythms
that come easy
effortlessly
like fastening earrings in the morning
natural   necessary
like wearing dresses on sunday
and in your remembering you come
quick   infinite
waterfall-like
the flow is habitual
like filling the coffeepot before studying
habitual   compelling   like reaching for a cigarette

you be from the street
a concrete sister
meticulously carved from the fertility of the south
you be struttin strong
struttin
with typewriter keys
struttin
with the words
with the feelings
as they be rolling
colliding
trying to reach your fingertips first

you see it all be wrapped up in your hands
and how womenfolk
be touchin   feelin
easing their way into your heart
and how when you walk
your feet be testifyin
and the dust that flies is your witness
and when you cry
your eyes are like weeping willows
whispering tribal chants to juju gods

mostly warm
mostly chocolate you be
you
the scent of annual church picnics
and saturday bake sales
mostly strong
mostly love
you be

‾‾
v v v v

WHEN THE LIMBS WAVE

after it is time
it shall be they
who'll answer my questions

i'll no longer have use
of human restrictions
and partial lovers
at the crest of my life
will be a rideable wave
the last tilt

fittin these feet
and my amazing amazonness

perfect
darkened by aged embraces
savored
for this moment only
when it is time
the trees will stand
and speak for me
in a voice reserved
for dethroned queens
and impulsive ladies

v v v v

BLINDED

i remember walking through the room
after mama had finished dressing
sitting by the window
sifting through
inhaling
the smells imposed upon the air

so many scents
i'd close my eyes and wish her there with me
chocolate from the cookies
she'd baked while we slept
sweetness from empty bottles of Chanel
gasoline and grass smells from the yard
that captured her free moments

long before the chocolate melted
and the sweetness went
i'd lift myself from the sill

drag my thoughts across the room
and quickly   quietly
close the door
so as not to lose her

‾‾‾
v v v v

WOMEN OF GLASS

there are mirrors
in my mother's house
and mirrors
in my own
in each room they cover
on so many walls they cling
our similarities
reflect each other
in tinted glass
and through brief glimpses of the other
our similarities
found only in these mirrors
which break so easily
unlike these women
who break so hard

‾‾‾
v v v v

BENEDICTION

for my uncle jack
who in an uneven thirty year
died

with gunshot holes his coat of armor
just outside ebenezer baptist
between a roll
with double sevens
still tight in his fist
though the family never discusses
the where of his final day
and continues to insist
it was our history of diseased hearts
and not the lucky sevens
though ebenezer is agreed upon
and our hearts
never stronger

ᵛ ᵛ ᵛ ᵛ

TRAMPOLINES AND QUEENS:
FOR VANESSA WILLIAMS

air
there are tiny
golden ripcords
hidden centerstage
between your esophagus
and adam's apple
that if you reach
and find
to pull
will save you
from a free fall
of any kind
from any source
in any season
ever
again

water
there are silver-centered
life-preservers
your size
bull's-eyed perfect
between your achilles
and little toe
that if you remember
to stand
perfectly still
and let fall tight around you
will pull you out
when you
make a wrong turn
and butterfly stroke
in a sidestroke-only race

land
there are
no name places
in your heart
where trampolines grow
and if you
jump there   trust there
know there are some of us
spotting for you
corner to corner
our arms
open
we
promise

FOLLICLES

dark and light
womenfolk
be doin hair
in the corners of used-to-be-pretty rooms
greased now with sulfur-eight smells
and hot-comb heat
womenfolk
dark and light
be havin hair done
slow
cause beauty ain't no easy thing
at 45
after children and men
and exploded dreams
have fallen at your feet
collected on your shoulders
and between your toes
like hair
from a shaven head
refusing to be brushed aside
womenfolk
dark and light
doing and having it done
sisters we paging you
wave your hand
so's we can get a proper count

FOR THE NEXT
ONE THOUSAND YEARS

*for the children of atlanta. for the children we claim who died. who are
dying. because they are Black. for our children. who thought the world
a silly playful place. where some only feared growing up. not explosions
in the midst of arithmetic. not the smell of ether where mommy's wet
kisses once were. for the children whose lives we claim and whose
deaths now claim us.*

in full we are paid
we owe nothing
on a bill that's never existed
the final payment is in
and for the next one thousand years
we are paid in full

for the last time they have grabbed us
snatched our lives
out in the open open
in places where t.v. cords won't reach
and microphones won't carry
out in the open open
where space holds us guarded
"somebody knows" they whisper
"somebody's seen"

chattahoochee
we have walked you old river
looking for the faces
curled and unwanted in your muddy breast
chattahoochee
broken prodigal stream
the mother river is looking for you
there are questions
and she is not proud

your eyes have seen these deaths
whisper their names to us
redeem yourself daughter stream
whisper now
and they won't know it was you
you owe them nothing   the bill's long been paid

and world
don't ever come to us again
heart in hand
hoof in mouth
ancient eyes in full bloom
don't even look this way
asking to be replenished
to be restocked
we are paid in full
for this
and for the next millenniums

incensed enough we are
until this world ends
and something else begins
paid up we are
tell your hands world
sign it out to your fingers
insist that your eyes remember
how this time
we have overpaid you

we owe nothing
no more
pass this word on
to the rivers behind you
for the next one thousand years
we are paid in full

〜〜〜

WRENCH FREE

it is never easy
to wrench free
the hands of a woman
who has just learned
how to hold
it is difficult
to convince her
that sleep will not steal it away

never is it easy
to make
she who has seen herself
only in animations
believe
she is not handing herself
to yet another dream

〜〜〜

WE ARE A NATION OF WOMEN

we are a nation of women
without those we want to love
without those we have heard
are good at loving
galaxies do not separate us
steel and bars and madnesses do
we are a nation of women
wishing
our eyes wander
as we work

our hearts roam
as we love
second-place lovers
that keep us
from those we really want
and loneliness
hunger drive us
to dangling ends
we cannot tie
we are an island
of deserted hearts
of unclaimed passions
left alone too long
we are a nation of women
answering ourselves
and wondering
if it's all right

∨∨∨

SUMTER 1967

i remember growing
and going to school
and mommy being patient
with my ungrownup ways
and each morning
before leaving her protectiveness
she'd encase silver gifts
in the knotted center of a small lavender cloth
for safekeeping
and after folding the willowiness of my ten years
into mothball-scented sweaters
her outgrown gloves
and a gray coat that bore the look of the generations

from whence it came
i was on my way

to dodge the dogs
that waited for the familiarity of my legs
to battle the wind
that sought to destroy my girlish softness
and to avoid
old lady aiken
who without failure
waited for me
goddess-like
on her uneven porch
swearing that on my pilgrimage to the sidewalk
i had touched the emerald green carpet that encased
her house

frightened and desiring the security of mommy's legs
i stood before her
rocking to the rhythm of the brisk morning breeze
and the steady crescendo of her eye movements
one hand twisting the longest braid
the other caressing the pages of a favorite book
listening
to the sparks that flew with each word
nodding my head respectfully
but not really listening

weeks passed and i learned her ways
i began leaving for school much earlier
before the sun had a chance to dance on her eyelids
and arouse an old afrikan temperament
that had lain dormant too long

FROM THE RAPTURE:
FOR THE WEATHER GIRLS

retrieved sisters
pulled
from the rapture
burned slightly
round edges only
no longer look back
for the fire that did not consume
no longer look hindways
in fear
heads no longer turn
when they enter the room
their feet can't find
the room to pivot
there is no direction
in which to flee anymore
arms
slightly scorched
on the inside
wave wildly
for more
still more
they dare to be burned again
only sisters
reprieved from the still-smoldering rapture
can rhapsodize

HOLDING FAST

crustacean-eyed uncles
long since dead
and met only now
through Polaroid's eyes
and the backsides of Kodak
you hang
all through my heart
no pins or yellowed adhesive
hold you there
   mule kisses
and moose hugs
hold you fast

TRIBAL MARKINGS

she had been sitting
singing about
losing something
i knew she never had
but still she sang
as if she knew
so i moved closer
and watched her
smooth oil
over dark and spotted knees
watched her
massage kitchen butter
across elbow scars

46

i scanned my own body
searched for similar tribal markings
that i knew were not there
but needed to see
as i was created in her image
and must carry
then pass
the traditional resemblances
of pain   of love   of relation
that should be there
between mothers   daughters
but was not
other than
the vertical lines
in our foreheads
that showed
when we smiled

no scars came
no spots
dark or otherwise
unattached i was
wanted to break
with the bond of my skin
intrude into its caramel silence
destroy the delicateness
of my life
become attached to her scars
an extension of her pain
first heir
to a trait
only we
could hold in common

THE TWENTIETH PSALM

grandmother
died at twenty
while giving birth to my father
while giving life
to her dream
she died of complications
formalities
they say
swept the south virginia breath
from her young body
sealed her eyes
before they had a chance to see
her creation
a simple woman
wanting only to be known
for the birth of a son
died penniless
of no great deeds
of no major accomplishments
simple
woman
succumbed to complications
and formalities
they say

CURRY IN THE MORNING

a jump rope hangs in the closet
behind an apron
worn and unfitting

                              they do not make aprons
                              for women of fourteen

a skate key
bound in cloth
lies next to the discolored gold band
she wears on occasions only

                              they no longer stock dreams
                              for women of fourteen
                              out of season
                              out of style
                              out of reach

she was against tying the knot
in the first place
but the eyes of her mother were constant
so she married him
for consistency's sake

sometimes she would ask about going out
anyplace
the answer was always no
so she'd return
to the back room the scent of the soap
and the security of the ironing board

                              fourteen
                              with no business
                              being a wife
                              but there are no rules
                              for women
                              who are mothers at fourteen

in the morning
she will reach past the apron
fondle the jump rope of her youth
and drape it around her neck

49

girl-scouting taught her
the proper way

and from its innocence
her life will dangle
a tribute to her creativity
and the girl scouts of america
on display for once
without his approval

‾‾‾
v v v v

OBSEQUIES:
FOR MA BEA

she buys only
the long wooden matches
hardest to find
easiest to last
refuses to discuss
which way
his hair should be brushed
and sashayed to his finality
tossing
the breath of peacocks
out of her eyes
and into the browning cornfields
he had left behind
a final gift
to her who had held his head
slept alone
changed his sheets
she refused to leave
his requiemed land
till the last shovel of warmth had been thrown

as eloquent as her entrance
a wedge of snuff
and savored saliva
the unquestionable adhesive
her sweet goodbye

―――
v v v v

IF YOU MUST WALK BY HIM
YOU DON'T HAVE TO LOOK DOWN

he has no legs
and so must move about
on knees
that must be feet as well as hands
selling peanut treasures
from a wagon
created first
for pulling dreams and sand dunes
created second
for towing children
not abnormalities
that have since turned into burdens
too difficult to carry
alone
the kind that cannot be left
in the yard
somewhere near a muddy puddle
at mommy's first beckon call for supper

SIAMESE TWINS

the right side
of the Red Dot store
and the colored funeral home's left
is joined in the center
they share a southern wall
lean deep into each other
as if there was no difference
in what each one kept cold

SIAMESE TWINS

the right side
of the Red Dot store
and the colored funeral home's left
is joined in the center
they share a southern wall
lean deep into each other
as if there was no difference
between misery and death

IF THEY DARE COME AT ALL

if they dare
come at all
certainly they will not stay long

not long enough for tea and berry pie
if they come
i won't let them
discover me
at 69
with my teeth out of place
and browning on the bureau
and my trunks
of uninterpreted poems
locked tight in the cellar
behind the scuppernong bottles
they will not
i won't let them
into my swollen house
and my dwindling life
past my suspicious cats
and into my parlor
if by then
the world has not heard
my voice
and understood
without retraction
then quietly
i will ask them to leave
before they ruin the carpet
and make a scene

‗‗‗
ⱽ ⱽ ⱽ ⱽ

ANNA

stalky feminine creature
a worldly woman
a maiden on a voyage all her own
to you my songs are sung

a thousand times in unison
as you go
understand the sea will be rough with you
but so too will you find its gentleness
tucked away
in the folds of each tide

Anna
maiden of the sea
on a voyage all her own
choreographing her own movements
sidestepping the small waves
bracing before those tall
it appears as if you came in on the wings of the moon
a maiden on a voyage
for a place unattended
after the storm
frosted in jade
and the scent of lemon peelings
there could never be another quite the same

‗‗‗‗
v v v v

CAMEL RIDERS

on the backs of trains they ride
like young purple sheiks
in a desert of steel
with reins made of air
deep pushed
into callused holding hands
that throw lantern light
like moonlight
back then forth
in front of us

who wave then wait
for them to pass
then turn a bend
riding from the hump
into no sunset
or rainbowed field
on the backs of trains they ride
prodigal sons
returning
to no fatted calves
and no fathers

v v v v

THE LEGEND OF WOMEN

cobalt-black
legend woman
of barely a brighter hue
your beauty beyonds exquisite

perfection opens
its cobwebbed door
to only you
and beckons in a tongue
unbeknown to all

       but she did not believe
       the first blood flow
       or the breaking of hymens
       would bestow
       womanhood's most cherished jewel
       in the last vacant spot
       of her crown

instead
she wrapped up well
from the waist down
went out into the world
and discovered
other sisters
emptying youth
deep into the swollen arms
of former mothers
who had since lost patience
with midnight feedings
and morning changes
frustrated
with not knowing
how or when
the best time
to indulge a dream

‾‾‾
vvvv

TWENTY-SIX THUNDERSTORMS

sometimes
i am an old woman
without tooth
or touch
as slow to change
as my hair is
to growing
fast
anymore

a mad woman
without kin
or kindness
screaming at
walls

for having faces and moving
doors
for having locks
and being closed

i am a dead woman
sometimes
buried
aboveground
in a thunderstorm
with all my things
and i lie there wondering
with my face all wet
can i go home now

v v v v

SAXOPHONE GRAY

old and blacker men
with hair that is not gray
or white
but moon pearl
and rare
old and blacker men
blow songs
make life
through tiny hollow holes
with soft easy mellifluous voices
that never stir or strike the air alone
but caress it soft
through saxophone gold
and blow songs
that do not make life easy
but make it good

ON WINGS MADE OF GAUZE

she lived not in a shoe
but on wings made of gauze
and when she left on midnight rides
she wrapped herself in moonbeams
to help light the way

her life before
had been tied to clotheslines
to shoestrings
of all sizes
of different hues
and after her life
no one cried
cause no one knew
how deeply her hands ached
and now when she's remembered
it's for the warm beer she guzzled
from tattered war canteens
and talk is still
how carelessly but gracefully
she flings them from the sky

in the evenings
if the light is right
quickly may you lift your eyes
and see her riding by
silhouetted by the moon
she rides boldly with no hands
as if life had no more boundaries
as if living held no more cautions

and in the mornings
if you walk quickly
before the others arrive
you may find one of her tattered canteens

scattered about the underbrush
and if you lift it gently to your lips
you'll find she didn't drink it all
she never does
she's left some for you
who've always been afraid of heights
and never had the courage
to fly

ABOUT THE AUTHOR

Nikky Finney was born in Conway, South Carolina, and graduated from Talladega College in Alabama. Her poetry has appeared in *Black Southerner Magazine, Callaloo Journal,* and elsewhere and has been included in anthologies published by the South Carolina Arts Commission, the Georgia Arts Commission, and in the Baltimore poetry anthology *Blind Alleys.* She is a member of the Pamoja Writing Collective, founded by Toni Cade Bambara. She presently works for the National Black Women's Health Project at the M. L. King Community Center in Atlanta, where she makes her home.